Elmer U. Hoenshel

The Land of Frost and Fire

Elmer U. Hoenshel

The Land of Frost and Fire

ISBN/EAN: 9783337254469

Printed in Europe, USA, Canada, Australia, Japan

Cover: Foto ©Andreas Hilbeck / pixelio.de

More available books at **www.hansebooks.com**

The Land of Frost and Fire

Partur af Arjágadri lyfsa lans á Akureyri.

Not in Florida, but on the Northern Coast of Iceland

THE LAND OF FROST AND FIRE

By
Elmer U. Hoenshel, D. D.

Author of
"My Three Days In Gilead,"
"By The Overflowing Nile," and
"The Crimson Trail."

THE McCLURE COMPANY, Inc.
Staunton, Va.

To My Father,

who, with strong physical prowess, and in unostentatious manner, battled for nearly a century of time to provide for his own, is inscribed this little volume.

THE AUTHOR.

Preface

In this volume I undertake to tell of what I saw in the "land of frost and fire." My tour will lead to a land not frequently visited by Americans, but nevertheless a land having many interesting features. In it I found many surprises awaiting me. And though the visit that I am to describe had in it much to annoy, yet it was full of experiences that I love to cherish in memory.

If by following the narrative as I tell it the reader may be able to live for awhile in the environment of the early Vikings and to appreciate the present-day struggles of a people that dwell in perpetual gloom for eight months of the year, then I shall be happy,—for my book will have performed the mission in whose interest I send it forth.

"ELRA OAKS," BASIC, VA.

Illustrations

Frontispiece
Bird-catching in the Faroes
In the Faroes
A Near View of Thorshavn
Thorstadur Farm House
Beautiful Falls at Seydisfjord
A Church at Husavik
A Herd of Horses
Loading Horses into the Boat
A Group: (1) Our Guide Arranging His Packs; (2) Mr. Walley, of England
A Fisherman's Luck
An Icelandic Farm
Haymaking in Iceland
Blonduos
A Group: (1) Steaming Hot Springs; (2) Guide and Dog; (3) Partially Dried Up Lake
A Group: (1) Loaded with Whale Meat; (2) Dranga Island; (3) Largest Tree seen by Author
A Fair Virginian in Ordinary Icelandic Dress
Icelandic Maiden, in Festive Attire
A Common Experience While Travelling in Iceland.
A Group: (1) On the Logberg; Thingvellir (2) Lake
The Almannagja
Hecla
A Scene in Reykjavik
West-mann Islands

Contents

Chapter	I.	"On the Way—The Faroes"	11
Chapter	II.	"The Land in General".	19
Chapter	III.	"The Eastern Fjords"	29
Chapter	IV.	"The Northern Fjords"	39
Chapter	V.	"Preparing for an Overland Trip"	48
Chapter	VI.	"Across the Island"	56
Chapter	VII.	"Second Day in the Interior"	68
Chapter	VIII.	"The Third and Fourth Day in the Interior".	75
Chapter	IX.	"The Valley of Thingvellir"	83
Chapter	X.	"Last Day on Horseback"	92
Chapter	XI.	"Reykjavik"	99
Chapter	XII.	"Good-By"	105

CHAPTER I

ON THE WAY—THE FAROES

ICELAND! Possibly the very name has caused the reader to shudder and to think that a land bearing such a designation should be shunned by any one seeking a pleasure-ground. But, without anticipating any essential feature of my story, I may now say that to such a one there are in store a number of pleasant surprises.

To see this land it was in my plan to make Leith, in Scotland, my starting-point. The date of my sailing was July 6, and this date was fixed and the fare paid several months in advance, even before my departure from America. The ship was scheduled to leave port at 11:00 a.m.

The morning set for my departure was filled with mist and gloom. And when I walked up the gang-plank of the *Botnia,* I was not pleased with the general appearance of the vessel that was to be my home for the greater part of a month. The crew had not yet finished coaling the boat, and the wet decks were filthy and un-

The Land of Frost and Fire

inviting. But I found my cabin and my berth much to my liking, even though my cabin-mate was a foreigner who could not speak or understand a word of my language.

The *Botnia* is a merchant-boat; but it also does a passenger-service, carrying about seventy-five people in addition to the crew. But the fact that the boat does a freight-traffic is favorable to the tourist, as it gives him sufficient time at the ports for him to make short excursions inland—sometimes as much as a half-day or more being given. The boat is 250 feet long and has a tonnage of only 1,206 tons; it is a small boat; and the smaller the boat, the bigger the sea—or at least, the bigger the effects of the sea. And since that northern ocean has a bad reputation I am half afraid and rather solicitous as to the trip.

Most of the passengers are foreigners to me. The crew are Danes. But few Englishmen and only three or four Americans are in the company.

We left port at 1:40 p.m.; moving slowly out through the maze of docks and shipping; and, reaching the open bay, we turned our prow northward and skirted the east coast of Scotland. The headlands and retiring firths present a constantly

The Land of Frost and Fire

changing panorama of beauty and interest. Already I note the late lingering twilight. To me the chief places of interest along this coast are the stacks, or needles, at Duncansby Head, and John O'Groat's House, the latter of which was for many years considered the most northerly habitation in Scotland. At present there are some houses still farther north. John O'Groat's house is in plain view from our boat; it is octagonal in form—and a Scotchman on board the vessel said that the house was so built that it might provide a part for each of Mr. O'Groat's eight sons who were constantly in hostile mood toward each other.

Having passed the northern point of Scotland in the night, the morning found us where we got the benefit of the full sweep of ocean winds and waves, and this made it very uncomfortable for me. Through the morning hours we passed the Orkney Islands, and while we were passing we found calmer seas. Beyond the Orkneys the voyage was quite rough, making my experiences the most miserable that I had as yet known at sea.

On the second morning we reached the Faroes. They looked picturesque in the early morning light—at 2:30 o'clock—and when we anchored a little later at Thorshavn, I was anxious to go ashore. We had careful boatmen, who soon landed us in safety.

These islands belong to Denmark. There are twenty-one of them, of which number seventeen are inhabited. The combined area is 514 square miles and the population is eleven thousand. The islands rise abruptly out of the water, and, since there is little or no tree growth, they present a desolate and forbidding aspect. Barley is the only cereal raised here. Peat and a poor grade of lignite coal constitute the chief fuel.

Thorshavn, the largest town in the entire group of islands, has a population of about two thousand, and, to a southerner, is quite odd in appearance. The streets are crooked and almost without pavements; half of the houses are sod-covered, and on many of them is an excellent crop of grass—as good as I saw on any of their lawns. These houses are first roofed with a layer of birch bark, and then covered with sod. Many houses have modern roofs, chiefly of iron.

Against the weather-boarding of a number of houses I saw mutton in the process of drying;

The Land of Frost and Fire

it looked so black and hard that I thought that surely it could never be eaten—but later, in Iceland, I saw such mutton served on the tables.

Here I visited the peat fields, and was surprised to find this kind of fuel so far north; but later I found it much farther north. Another surprise was the hearing of a lark—at least the song was like the song of a lark. In the high school, which I visited, I found the headmaster very respectful, and his pupils courteous in the extreme—removing their hats and standing at proper distance with uncovered heads while I was in the quadrangle.

At this port codfish are caught in abundance. And when they are split open (usually the work of the women), and spread on the rocks and shed-roofs to dry, the shore about Thorshavn presents a white appearance as seen from the sea. It was thus when I visited the place. Bird-catching, in season, is also one of the chief industries of the Faroese. Some fine buildings, fairly well stocked stores, and excellent telephone service are to be found in this town.

In general, the people look healthy, but many have a careworn expression on their faces. Among

The Land of Frost and Fire

the women I saw some who were passing fair. Everybody is courteous—even the children lifting their hats in greeting. The women wear lambskin slippers over which they wear wooden soles having heels. The temperature here was not colder than I had experienced earlier in the season in Scotland.

Leaving Thorshavn about noon we proceeded through the narrow straits among the islands, which are sometimes so beautiful, and next stopped at Klaksvig for a couple of hours in the afternoon. At this port was the climax of interesting scenery in the Faroes. Then we passed on to the open sea.

As we left the Faroes, a beautiful view of needles and a tunneled island was afforded us. At 8:30 o'clock next morning, we entered a heavy fog which lasted until 9:30 o'clock in the evening. Frequently the fog was so dense that the range of vision was limited to fifty yards, or less, in every direction. All day we moved slowly and cautiously on, the fog horn giving out continually its notes of warning. Frequent soundings were made to determine depth and location. The latter is determined by having tallow on the end

Bird-catching in the Faroes

In the Faroes

A Near View of Thorshavn

The Land of Frost and Fire

of the plummet, so that when the plummet strikes the bottom of the sea sand will adhere to the tallow. This sand is taken to the captain who studies it in connection with his chart of the bottom of the sea, and by so doing is able to tell with accuracy the position of his boat. In the forenoon we heard the warning signal of another vessel that was plowing its way somewhere in the sea-mist—it seemed like some great animal in distress. At two o'clock in the afternoon I saw a twenty-foot whale not more than ten yards from our boat. At nearly four o'clock a whaling vessel suddenly appeared within our little mist-encircled world, like a phantom ship out of the clouds; after a short conversation was held by the captains it disappeared as mysteriously as it came. The sun tries to pierce the mist-laden atmosphere, but it rests like a pall over the sea; and slowly we move on into mystery. Thrice we make circles of small diameter, in the movement of our vessel, in order to be sure that our compass is not erring in its service.

Later there came back an echo to our warning call, and then we knew that we were near land. It was evident that if the veil were to lift a

The Land of Frost and Fire

beautiful panorama of southern Iceland would be ours. But it showed no signs of lifting. So the machinery of the vessel was stopped. And while we lay idly waiting for the fog to lift, some of the passengers played ring-toss, but the Faroese on board plied their life vocation—they began at once to fish; and notwithstanding the water was over a hundred feet deep they caught some large cod.

But while we wait for the sky to clear, let us make a brief general study of the land at whose portal we lie waiting for nature's permission to enter, so that when we thread its fjords and tread its fields and fens we shall be on ground with which we are already familiar.

CHAPTER II

The Land in General.

The land on whose shore we wait hidden in sea-mist lies just on the edge of the Artic Circle, 250 miles from Greenland and 600 miles from Norway. It belongs geographically to the western hemisphere, but historically and politically to the eastern. Having an area of 39,200 square miles, it is nearly as large as Kentucky. Its entire population is scarcely over seventy thousand. Iceland is of volcanic origin; its rocks are almost all igneous; and there are yet several active volcanoes, the chief of which is Hecla, over five thousand feet high. Therefore, it is fittingly called a "land of fire." In its elevations are presented many kinds of scenery and climatic conditions. Much of the island is perpetually covered with snow and ice—one jokul, the Vatna, having in itself an area of four thousand square miles. (A "jokul" is a mountain or high plateau that is never free from its ice covering). Hence this land is also fittingly called a "land of frost."

The summers in Iceland are short, and warm

The Land of Frost and Fire

considering the latitude; the winters are long and cold, yet tempered somewhat by the Gulf Stream. For four months in the year the stars do not shine, and for four months the sun does not shine. Thus the year in Iceland may be thought of as one long day—four months light, four months night, four months twilight.

Strange as the assertion may seem, it is said that two-thirds of the population are farmers. But since no cereal can be matured here because of the shortness of the season, the farmers devote themselves to the cultivation of short-season vegetables and grass, and to the raising of stock. The horse, sheep, cow, dog, and cat are their domestic animals. Live-horses, wool, tallow, and fish-oil are the chief products and articles of export.

Seven thousand men are engaged in the fisheries of the country. And the story of daring and privation of these fishermen in a single season would stir the hearts of the thousands in America who think their own struggle for a living a hard one.

The only wild animal is the fox, and it is becoming rare. High in the interior a few reindeer may be found; but tourists seldom see

The Land of Frost and Fire

them. Of birds the raven, the falcon, the ptarmigan, the curlew, and the eider-duck are the most noted. I saw not many ravens. The falcons to-day are few; but it is the national-bird of Iceland, as is the eagle for America. At one time they were numerous here and were exported to the countries of southern Europe for the use of hunters in the chase, organized, or otherwise. The falcon is a bird of prey, like a large hawk in appearance and habits. It can be trained to soar aloft to sight game and then to swoop down quickly to catch and hold it for the hunter. "Hawking," as it was called, was a favorite pastime a few centuries ago, in which the falcon took the place of trained dogs.

As just stated, the falcon is the national emblem, and its representation is seen on flags, and in devices over the doorways to public buildings, and is used extensively on pins and brooches.

The curlew is a bird that interests at first; but, because of its peculiar mocking cry, it becomes a menace to the peace of the traveler overland. The eider-duck is of a brownish-gray color, and its down, not plucked from the bird but gathered from its nest after the young are hatched, is valuable in commerce.

The Land of Frost and Fire

Upon returning from my tour in Iceland there were those who asked me if the island were not peopled with Eskimo! And some asked if they were not savages! Such questions as these frequently repeated cause me to know that information concerning this interesting land is very vague; and it is an inducement for me to put in print my knowledge gained in the land itself.

That you may know the Icelander as seen and studied by men capable of expressing opinion, I quote from a paper by Prof. James Mavor, prepared in 1891 and read before the Philosophical Society of Glasgow in that year:

"The Icelanders are not wholly barbarous; on the contrary they are supremely civilized. They are among the most expert horsemen, the best caligraphists, the best printers, the best archaeologists, the best makers of coffee in the world; and if these accomplishments were not enough, they are musical, learned, and courteous, and their moral tone is distinctly higher than that of any other people in Europe."

This high moral plane is probably due not so much to careful religious training as to the "absence of any desire for display and emulation,

The Land of Frost and Fire

and to the prevailing simplicity of life and the rudimentary development of luxury."

Their intimate family association—all members of the family ordinarily occupying the same bed-chamber, and even guests, at times, compelled by circumstances to share a place in the same room—would suggest to us shocking, if not immoral conditions. But no such thought ever seems to enter the Icelander's mind. The women of the home take care of the guest with a modest simplicity that commands admiration and semi-reverence for the sex. In innocency and artless, open manner they seem like grown up children.

It is said that one custom, known in primitive marriage lore as "hand-parting," yet prevails to an extent in Iceland. It is this: "A man and a woman contract to live together for a year. If at the end of the year, the parties agree thereto, they are married; if not, they separate without stigma on either side. The contract may be made conditionally binding from the first; it may bind the parties to marry in the event of issue, or in the event of no issue, as the case may be."

For centuries the educational work was done

almost exclusively by the ministry of the land, and in the interior it is so done to-day. But it is said that the public-school system is good; that not a child over ten years old can be found that cannot read, and that many of the peasants are proficient in the classic languages. There are a number of newspapers printed in Iceland, in one of which I saw a unique way of printing a continued story. At the bottom of the page was printed in nicely and carefully arranged and paged columns, on both sides of the sheet, the installment of the story for that issue. By cutting out, and preserving each installment, until the story is finished, there is only need to fold and stitch the sheets together and the book is complete, except that it lacks a back. I had never seen such arrangement elsewhere.

Yes, they are courteous to strangers and to each other to a degree that I have not seen excelled, if equaled, in any other land. And at no time in my experiences in Scandinavian countries did I see any one indicate a desire for a gratuity. (In southern Europe just the opposite is true.)

I quote further from the paper already re-

The Land of Frost and Fire

ferred to: "The Icelander is a creature pursued by frost and fire. His short summer is a time of incessant toil, and his long winter a period of shivering inaction. The gloom of the eight months of winter, the perpetual desolation of a vast part of the whole island, the frequent storms that make the life of a fisherman on the coast a series of campaigns in which the dead are many and the living few; the toilsome cultivation of sterile soil, the prevalence of disease due to exposure, these are reasons sufficiently potent to account for the strain of subdued sadness in Icelandic manners. It is no wonder that the Icelander is deficient in humor. Life to him is a tragedy—the comic element is crushed out in the stress of a hard-won and a hard-kept existence."

It is said that the Icelander has but few games, and that until quite recently the children had no dolls or toys. You hear little hilarity about the homes or on the streets. But enough of this for the present; we shall know the people and their land better when I have finished my story.

My sketch of the history of Iceland will be very brief. It was anciently known as Thule. In the eighth century the Culdees were in the

The Land of Frost and Fire

land. In 866 A.D., a Norse Viking by the name of Raven Floke spent the winter there, a sort of prisoner behind ice-barriers; and it is said that he gave the land the name that it bears to-day. In 874, Ingolf and Lief settled, or founded, Reykjavik. Because of tyrannical measures by Harald Fairhair, king of Norway, many of his subjects emigrated to Iceland and joined Ingolf and Lief in their new settlement. Two hundred and fifty years after the founding of Reykjavik, Iceland had a population of fifty thousand people.

The Althing was formed in 930 and lasted for several hundred years as the government of the land; it met for two weeks every summer at Thingvellir. While it was in session laws were made, cases tried, and sentences executed. In the year 1,000, the Althing made Christianity the religion of Iceland. And with the liberation of the intellect there began to develop a literature. It was the age of the *Sagas*, (family legends and traditions) and of the *Eddas*, (productions similar to the *Sagas*, but more poetical).

The development of feuds and internecine strifes led to Iceland's becoming subject to

The Land of Frost and Fire

Norway in 1264. In 1380, Norway with Iceland became subject to Denmark, and remained so until 1814. In that year Norway went over to Sweden, but Iceland still remained subject to Denmark. In 1874, the thousandth anniversary of Iceland's history, the king of Denmark attended their great celebration at Thingvellir, and on that occasion granted the island complete home rule; though she is still recognized as a Danish possession.

The modern government is composed of a Governor and a Congress consisting of two chambers, or houses. Six members of Congress are appointed by the king of Denmark and thirty members are elected by the people. This Congress is to-day called by its ancient name, the Althing.

Iceland has no army or munitions of war; nor is any military service required of the people. It is said that in 1910 there were only ten policemen on the island; and that for a good part of the time there is not a prisoner in any jail.

These people have taken advanced steps relative to the liquor question. They saw how the strength of their people was failing through

The Land of Frost and Fire

strong drink and they rose to meet the emergency. In September, 1908, they voted on the question of prohibition for Iceland with the following result: For prohibition 4,645 votes were cast; against prohibition there were 3,181 votes. The measure carried with a majority of 1,464 votes. Then they passed a law prohibiting the importation of intoxicants, such law to take effect on January 1, 1912, and prohibiting the sale after January 1, 1915. The following is quoted from their bill relative to ships doing business in her ports,—"All ships must have their liquors under seal from the time they are three miles from land, and the ships must not sell liquors to passengers inside this limit."

Of course, it is not new to the intelligent reader that Iceland claims the honor of discovering our country about five hundred years before the visit of Columbus. And thus they teach their children. The records seem to be in favor of the "children of the Vikings," so let them be happy in claiming this great honor.

CHAPTER III

THE EASTERN FJORDS.

But to take up the story as left off at the close of the first chapter. Our boat lay idle in the fog until after nine o'clock that evening. Then we began to see the dim outlines of mountains appearing through the dissipating mist. But it required some time before the captain could definitely locate us. When all had cleared we found ourselves near the coast, and that we had passed a little way beyond the mouth of the fjord that we wished to enter.

While passing up the fjord I see for the first time a whaling station. But the object that I see anchored to a buoy and floating there is not a large row-boat bottomside up—it is a whale nearly or quite fifty feet in length.

Eskifjord, the fjord that we are now entering, is my introduction to that peculiar feature of northern scenery known as fjords. A fjord (pronounced as though an "i" were substituted for the "j" and then considered as one syllable), as I would describe it, after seeing scores in those high latitudes, is a land-locked bay, usually very narrow and deep, many of them extending in angled or serpentine course far inland with high precipitous walls of rock on either side.

On this evening, when the fog lifted, a beautiful panorama of sea and land stretched out before us. The waters of the fjord were quiet and restful to us after rocking all day in our mist-draped "cradle of the deep." Here and there on the upward sloping land I could see a farm with some domestic animals browsing about in the open; higher up I saw snow.

As the evening wore on a strange silence fell on the passengers, all of whom stood—just looking. I seemed to be all eyes and emotions as I stood on deck in the bright after-glow, at nearly eleven o'clock p.m., while we steadily pushed on into the quiet fjord which seemed sentineled by majestic mountains standing guard in quiet. It seems to me like a dream-visit to a dream-island, and the low-toned voices of those about me seem at times coming out of the shadowy past. I look upon the brown-ledged mountain walls with snow-patches in depressions, in some places even as low

The Land of Frost and Fire

down as the water line. Numerous streams find their way down the slopes—some with steady flow, others in cascades and cataracts with splashing and foaming rebound. When the heights with their jagged skyline and snow-flecked sides were kissed by the lingering light of a day that here scarcely knows death, and the soft somber shadows took on lilac and roseate hues, it was like a bit of heaven, I think, lent to guide us into the port of the great home of light and peace.

When we reached Eskifjord, the town at the head of the fjord of the same name, it was nearly midnight, although it was still light enough to read ordinary newspaper print. We anchored about two hundred yards from the shore, and while we lingered some of the passengers went for a little trip on land. The town has only about fifty houses, and they are strung along the water's edge. At a large building an auction, or general distribution of goods, was in progress—it presented an interesting pantomimic sight as viewed from the boat. It seemed much like a shadowgraph performance, for all was quiet except a low murmur of voices at times. Near Eskifjord

The Land of Frost and Fire

are the richest and best mines of Iceland Spar in the world. One of the joint owners of the mines brought some fine specimens of the spar on board and exhibited its peculiar property of double refraction; and since he joined our cruise at this point he took occasion to tell a few times of the worth of the mines, and referred with pride to his anticipated wealth when the mines would be fully developed.

At 6 a.m. we left this port. The trip out of the fjord was scarcely less interesting than was the going in. On reaching the open sea we again encountered fog and had to make our way slowly northward along the coast until we reached the mouth of Seydisfjord, at the head of which was our next port of call, and which we reached at 11 a.m. This fjord is about twelve miles long, the upper portion being quite out of sight of the sea. "The rocks on one side of the fjord are like wild castellated ruins, on the other side the mountains are higher and are dotted with glaciers." About a quarter of a century ago an avalanche from impending crags cut the village in two.

The town of Seydisfjord is said to rank fourth

Thorstadur Farm House

Beautiful Falls at Seydisfjord

A Church at Husavik

The Land of Frost and Fire

in size of the towns in Iceland. It has a population of about a thousand people. In it there are a splendid school building, a hospital, and a number of up-to-date looking stores and homes. I was surprised to find so many frame houses in a land where there are no trees for timber or lumber. On our approach we noted an unusual display of national colors and emblems. Many flags were seen unfurled on buildings; and provision for the hoisting of flags was seen on almost every house of note in the town. The people seemed very patriotic—proud of their "land of frost and fire."

On reaching the pier the captain told us that the vessel would not leave until five o'clock that evening. Several miles inland are the beautiful Skogafoss falls; but as it is Sunday, I prefer not to make the trip, but rather to go to church and quietly to study the people and that wonderful environment that largely made them what they are. So, in company with two Englishmen, I start to find the church. I pass around the head of the fjord, cross a dashing glacier-torrent, move on through the town by the fish-drying areas, and then follow a foot-path down the other side of the fjord, until, four miles from the boat, I find the village church. In passing through the town I noted the people. Many of the females are fairly pretty and dress with neatness. Usually they wear their hair in long curls or braids down the back. Many of them wear the lambskin shoes or slippers. The men wear similar footwear, but often over the slippers they wear low wooden shoes. Some of the men here wear knee-breeches with brass buttons. The tendency in color of hair is light—a sort of rusty yellow—though some have black hair.

The three of us found the church, but in it were only two men—the preacher and the chorister, both in the choir loft. Later a woman came and left. Then the preacher left. The building in its exterior and interior would not be a disgrace to any rural community in our country. It belongs to the Lutheran denomination. There is scarcely any other faith represented on the whole island. Finally the chorister came down to apologize; we couldn't understand what he said, but we knew what he meant. We wanted some kind of service, so we took him back to the choir loft and persuaded him to play and sing some of the music used in their services. We found it harder to get him to stop than to get him to begin. But it was interesting to us.

After singing a couple of English hymns for him we went down to the door of the church. The day was ideally beautiful. We heard a rushing roaring as of waterfalls somewhere near; but we could not see them. Beautiful falls, five hundred or a thousand feet high could be seen across the fjord, but this sound did not come from them. In trying to find the source of this nature-music coming out of the mountain-side we began climbing up the steep slope, picking our way over grassy swards where purple columbine, buttercups, and saxiphrage were blooming. Thus we continued for half an hour or so, and then we stood on the edge of a deep chasm in the side of the mountain, in which rushing and fighting its way down the fjord was a stream of medium size fed by the perpetual snow a little higher up. Selecting a strategic view-point from which three falls in the stream proper and two smaller ones in a tributary are in the range of my vision, I sit on the grass, pluck flowers, look,

The Land of Frost and Fire

listen, meditate. And while I watch a beautiful rainbow spans the ever-ascending mist.

It is warm; the temperature in the shade is 70 degrees F. by the thermometer we have with us. Wild flowers about me! And this is Iceland!

As I sit under the noise of the roaring of these five falls, I think of that awful struggle in a death chamber, just nine years ago almost to the hour, when they said concerning my mother—"she is dead." And the thought induces anew a feeling of sadness and loneliness. But when I look upon the beautiful rainbow swinging radiant over the symbol of destruction it becomes a messenger of cheer to me. Storms and stress may prevail in the world, but over all, and occasioned in part by them, hope, peace, and rest in the sweet after while are written in the iris-hued angel-path of the bow.

Then we go a little farther up to the snow, where in good natured fashion we snowball each other and slide or skate over the hard crust, and then land almost in the midst of wild flowers! Then we return to the boat, where in the warm summer breath of that evening I put away my

The Land of Frost and Fire

flowers, and enclose one in a letter with instructions to place it, though withered, on the grave of her who was willing to go into the "valley of the shadow" that I might live.

We left Seydisfjord at 7 p.m., two hours later than the expected hour for loosing from the pier. After a pleasant sail of four hours we found ourselves at the mouth of Vopnafjord. It was 11 p.m. and the sun was just disappearing below the horizon. And just as the sun set the cloud obscuration was such as to present for some minutes the exact representation of a golden boat skimming along on the surface of the sea.

The little town of half a hundred houses is soon reached and then some of the passengers go ashore. But I prefer to remain on the boat to read and to watch the heavens until the sun should appear again—this it did at half-past one o'clock. The changing glory of the sea, land, and sky in those two and a half hours is beyond description.

Across the fjord at this point the cliffs are very high and have large patches of snow on them. On these the after-glow kept playing in changing hues and tints until a purplish brown,

The Land of Frost and Fire

or chocolate, was reached at the moment of deepest shadow (but still it was light enough for one to read fine print), and then changed again and again so subtly that the royal light of a new day was shining full on the snowy crests before I was aware of its sure approach. And the golden glory of the northern sky! Bare your heads and be silent, in this land of silences! A heavenly gold-dust fills the whole atmosphere!

I am now ready to retire, but it is not to immediate sleep.

Experiences such as these make one reverent. God is here.

CHAPTER IV

The Northern Fjords.

We weighed anchor at Vopnafjord at 7:00 a. m. On reaching the sea we again encountered a heavy fog that lasted until about 3:00 p. m., and during that time we rounded the extreme northeastern part of Iceland and were for a short time within the Arctic Circle. But though so far north the temperature ranged at about seventy degrees Fahrenheit, and for a while stood at eighty degrees. The air was summer-like. At 6:00 p. m., we reached Husavik, our next port of call, and here nearly all the passengers went ashore.

Most of the houses at Husavik are modern in construction and some homes are surrounded with pretty lawns—now so green. And flowers abound. There were acres of yellow buttercups. I never saw a more luxuriant growth of rhubarb anywhere. Currants were half-matured. Here was an excellent church with very fine exterior, and above the altar was an old painting

The Land of Frost and Fire

of regarded merit. The telephone service was quite commendable. Caravans of horses were seen in the town, and some were coming from the interior, and still others were returning to the interior. Here were sunshiny children, rather somber looking men, and some attractive girls sitting on the porches or on the rich grass of the lawns in summer dress—presenting a scene not unlike what might be observed on a May evening in the Valley of Virginia—and yet it was on the northern shore of Iceland, within a few miles of the Arctic Circle. The fisher-folk were busy drying cod—the harvest of their labor at sea.

We left Husavik at about 9.00 p. m., with a half-assurance from the captain that we might get a glimpse of the *midnight sun* if the weather conditions were favorable; but we were a few days too late in the season for us to see the sun at midnight. But as I shall go next month as far north of Iceland as Iceland is north of London, I feel sure of seeing the phenomena there that I missed seeing here. But still this night was by no means a disappointment to me—there

A Herd of Horses

Loading Horses into the Boat

Guide Arranging His Pack   Mr. Walley, of England

A Fisherman's Luck

The Land of Frost and Fire

was so much color-beauty, enhanced even by the clouds.

Sometime in the early morning we tied to the excellent pier at Akuereyri. At all other ports, except Seydisfjord, we had to cast anchor and then go ashore in row-boats. Here we may walk down a gang-plank. And here we shall lie all day.

This town is second in size of the towns of Iceland, having a population of nearly two thousand people. In Akuereyri there are two or three fairly good streets, a fine hotel, splendid stores, and beautiful homes—a number of the houses having art-glass windows. When we went to secure the services of a telephone we found the equipment quite up to date—the offices even being supplied with a tape-recording machine. I note but little smoking among the men, and uniform courtesy prevails. The men on parting are sometimes seen to kiss each other. Buttercups, violets, wild thyme, and asters are here in profuse abundance. The largest tree that I saw in the whole island is here; it is only about twenty feet high, and stands in the dooryard of one of the homes. The people of the town are quite proud of it.

The Land of Frost and Fire

Modern manner of locomotion is also recognized here, for I saw one carriage and two bicycles.

In the evening, I walked up a grassy ravine that was lined upon both sides with houses to where hay-making was in progress. The grass was short, but very dense in growth. It is what is called native grass, like our American blue grass—it needs to be fertilized, but not resown. 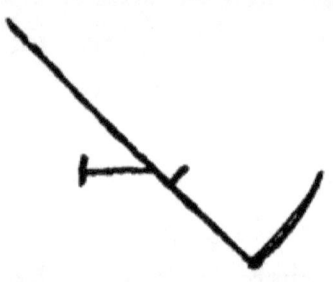 The scythe is of peculiar construction and is used in a vigorous downward stroke very unlike anything I have ever seen used in mowing. I did not try to use the scythe.

Next I passed over to a field where a man was engaged in making meadow-land. Nearly all the arable land-surface of Iceland is covered with little hummocks of irregular shape and size. To mow such land is very tedious; but they have been doing it for centuries. They literally shave these hummocks, for every blade of grass is valuable in Iceland. Some of them seem to think that there is an easier way to harvest the

The Land of Frost and Fire

grass than by trimming and shaving the hummock-covered meadows; and so they are making the surface level. Where this man was working he had stripped off all his sod and had heaped it on piles at the side of his small plot; then he had leveled down the hummocks, and had covered the surface with a layer of dead fish—fish that were too small for value in commerce, but had been caught in the nets along with the better fish. This covering was for fertilizer. Then he replaced the sod.

When I approached the man I had to walk over the fish-covered ground, and the stench was awful! Sea gulls were hovering about in great number, like flies near a carcass. To the surprise of the workman, I walked up to him, took his crude shovel and laid a wheelbarrow load of sod for him. When I returned the shovel he smiled, bowed, and quietly said, *"Tahk,"* (thank you).

Then I passed down to the town to go aboard the vessel. But before going to the boat it was a beautiful sight to watch the children playing with the wild-flowers that bloom so profusely here. They had their hands full of violets and had wreaths of wild thyme hanging over their shoulders or made into bracelets. One little girl on seeing my interest courteously removed a wild thyme bracelet from her dainty wrist and held it out smilingly to me as an offering. And when I took it she tripped gaily back to her associates. To-day I prize the little memento of her kindness above many other things whose intrinsic values are far greater.

Before we loosed from the pier over one hundred and fifty live horses had been loaded onto our boat and stabled in the hold. They were swung up one at a time to a point over the open hatchway and then lowered quickly to their place in the hold. Icelandic horses usually are pretty; they are small, but somewhat larger than the Shetland pony. On our rough voyage back to Scotland the presence of these horses and the hundred more that were loaded at Reykjavik did not add any pleasure to our experiences.

That night was most beautiful. The sun sank below the horizon at about twenty minutes of twelve o'clock, and the afterglow was most gorgeous, even lighting up the spray-drops caused by the movement of our boat until they looked like little globes of amethyst. And I never before saw such blue in clouds—and such gold—and such cloud-shapes! The sun was below the horizon not more than an hour.

Early on the following morning we stopped a few hours at Kolkuos, well up in Skagaffjord. At the mouth of this fjord is Dranga Island. This island is of interest because about 700 years ago, as recorded in a *Saga,* an outlaw by the name of Grettir, a Samson in strength and daring, when fleeing from Iceland made it his home and held it for several years against the attacks of the government to take him. But he was finally overcome. The island is very high and has a flat, grassy top with a area of about a square mile. But the sides rise so abruptly from the sea that it is almost impossible to scale them. A great fissure which can be plainly seen from one viewpoint almost completely cuts the island in two. It is said that 80,000 birds are killed annually at this island. Near it is a picturesque rock chimney, or needle, rising many feet (maybe as many as a hundred feet), out of the sea.

The Land of Frost and Fire

At Sauderkrok, a town of about seventy houses, just at the head of this same fjord, I went ashore at 11:00 a. m. The "villa nova" is the most beautiful home here, and its hostess is a queen in bearing and courtesy. She brought out eider-down for me to see, after I had manifested interest in the eider-ducks that were at this place. This seems to be quite a business town. The farmers are bringing in their wool; it must be carried on their little horses, but still the packs are large. The sacks are tied on the panniers with ropes that the natives have made out of the manes of their horses. Rings for harness are made from sheep's horns. They also utilize fish bones to good purpose. The farmers take whale-meat, flour, and other supplies for their long dreary winter back into the interior in exchange for the wool.

At Sauderkrok there is no grassy sward as at the other towns we have visited. The houses skirt the sandy, rocky shore. But I climb the heights just back of the village, rising one hundred feet or more above sea-level, where I found men at work in a cemetery. Approaching them I saw a coffin already in the grave that they were

The Land of Frost and Fire

digging, and that they were digging besides the first corpse to make room for another to take his long rest on the hill above the site of his life-struggle to live. The view from this height—above the quiet fjord—is one of rare beauty. May the tenants of this, "God's acre," have rest from their labors!

Weighing anchor at 3:00 p. m., we pass around into the next fjord, by the wreck of the *Laura,* of this same steamship line, and stop at Skagastrond for six hours. On leaving Skagastrond at 2:30 a. m., I am in high expectations, for it is only a little way to the next port and when we have reached it, then "good-by" for a week to the *Botnia,* for I have planned to go across the island on horseback instead of going on around by boat.

CHAPTER V.

Preparing for an Overland Trip

In Sailing around Iceland one can see much of beauty and interest, but one can have but little knowledge of the interior of the island by staying on board the vessel, or even by going ashore at the coast towns and villages. So a number on board the *Botnia* planned to go into the interior by crossing the island; but all so doing did not leave the boat at the same port.

I wanted to cross the island. I wanted to see the life and customs that are practically unchanged since the days of Grettir, Gisli, Sigmund, and the other heroes of the *Sagas*. But as there was no other way by which to go than on horseback I shrank from the undertaking. But an intelligent and companionable Englishman, Thomas Walley by name, was also especially anxious to go; and since he desired only one companion other than the guide, the arrangement appealed to me, and I soon found myself eagerly planning with him for the trip; and had our plans failed to materialize, as

An Icelandic Farm

Haymaking in Iceland

The Land of Frost and Fire

did the plans of some, I would have been as bitterly disappointed as he, even though such failure to go would have meant deliverance from much suffering that was to come. Our minds were definitely made up when we reached Akuereyri. At that place, with some help from interpreters, we had succeeded in getting reply to a telephone message sent on to Blonduos. We had sent word for a guide to meet us at the landing with six horses, ready for a trip across Iceland to Reykjavik. The answer had come back that we would be met by a trusty guide, in whom we could place every confidence—but one who could not speak a word of English. It was not to our liking, but since now it was this or no overland trip, we had sent word back that everything should be in readiness for us at the arrival of the boat.

We thought we could reach the landing-place by midnight, but we were late; and the hour of our arrival being uncertain, we did not retire. So the night passed without our getting any sleep. Later, we hoped we would not reach port until after breakfast, for we knew that on the boat we should fare well—yonder in the little village of Blonduos was uncertainty as to a palatable meal. But at five o'clock in the morning we reached the place of anchoring, and then we had to leave the vessel. Not expecting to find English-speaking people here, we asked the resident German Consul of Iceland, a native of the island, and who himself was a passenger on the boat, to accompany us ashore and to give our guide all the instructions that we had to offer. This gentleman was glad to go and help us; and he prepared to accompany us with manifest courtesy and kindness of manner. Then we said good-by to our friends on the *Botnia,* hoping to see them a week later at Reykjavik.

The name of the consul was Thomsen. And here I digress to call attention to the peculiarity of Icelandic names. The children do not take the family name of their parents, but the Christian name of the father becomes the surname of the child. To illustrate: Our overland guide's name was *Pall Jansson* (Paul Johnson); this meant that his own name was Paul, that he was John's son, therefore, Paul John's son (Pall Jansson). Further, had he a brother by the name of Eric, that brother's full name would be Eric John's son (Eric Johnson). And had he a sister whose name was Helga, her full name would be Helga John's daughter (Helga Jansdottir). And had he himself a son whose first name was Lief, his full name would be Lief Paul's son (Lief Pallsson).

And so it happened when I wrote down the name of the consul as I was accustomed to spell the name, he, looking over my shoulder, pointed to the last syllable and said, "Spell it *s-e-n.*" I said, "Why?" He answered, "My name is Thom*sen;* I am not *Thom's son.*" And then I understood.

When our little boat reached the shore no one in the village was stirring, except two or three persons who were waiting on the pebbly beach to take care of any freight that might be landed. We had left behind all unnecessary luggage, so needed no helpers. In company with Mr. Thomsen, the consul already referred to, we walked up the sandy slope and into the little village. After winding around through a few alleyways and back yards, we fronted a fine residence with shell-bordered walk leading to the front porch and having flower beds on both sides of it. Here lived the man who had phoned to us about our trip—so said the interpreter. Then we all tried to wake the occupants, but failed. The consul left us to attend to some business on the other side of the Blanda, a river of considerable size, flowing into the fjord at this place.

Mr. Walley and I watched the house alternately and simultaneously, now and again knocking to get recognition. Then as the morning wore on the thought of a good breakfast caused us to make a search for food. But nothing could be found until about eight o'clock, when a man *half* opened his store—he was not open for business, but I went in. I could find nothing to eat, except some stale sugar cakes—not fit to eat. We gave up the search.

And just about that time our sound sleeper awoke. And though he had arranged for our trip he could not talk English. But our interpreter has returned. After holding a short conversation with this man, he tells us that the guide has been engaged for our service, that he lives a few miles inland, and that he was in the village the evening before to make inquiry concerning the arrival of the boat; and that all we could now do was to wait. But we had already been in port

The Land of Frost and Fire

three hours, and we did not know how soon the boat would call our interpreter from us. But at that moment a man came down the hill-path leading to the village riding like Jehu. His horse stopped suddenly and he was off like an automaton and stood before us looking interest. Yes, it was our guide—a man about thirty years of age, five feet and ten inches tall, and well proportioned physically. His face was red, but pleasing, giving assurance of honesty and good-will.

Through the consul we quickly came to an understanding. Our guide was to furnish six horses (but for emergency he said he'd take along an extra horse at his own expense); he was to take us over the route that we had designated; he was to show us things of special interest along the way; he was to secure lodging and food for us; and he was to make the trip in such time as to reach Reykjavik a day or two before the scheduled time for the departure of the *Botnia* for Scotland.

He soon agreed to all this, shaking his head at some of the things that we wanted to do, and which later we were glad to eliminate from our list of things to be seen. It was agreed to that we should pay him six kroner a day for his services, and two kroner a day for each of the six horses, making our obligation to him eighteen kroner (about $5.00) a day. And we were to pay him at the same rate for his return, which he estimated would require about two days less time than the outward trip. We were to pay for our lodging and food; he was to provide food and lodging for himself and horses.

Then I had a request to make. I said to Mr. Thomsen, "Tell the man that I want an easygoing horse, and I want a comfortable saddle, and I want him to put a sheepskin on my saddle, and *I want the woolly side up!*" He agreed to it, and smiled. Then all having been arranged for, as we thought, the consul gave us an interested good-by, hoping that we would enjoy our trip through the land that meant home to him, and after a cordial inviation to call upon him in Reykjavik, and some further admonition to the guide, he returned to the boat whose warning signal for departure had already been given.

Our guide sprang to his beast and was away like a flash to get the horses that were being "rounded up" in his absence. In half an hour he

The Land of Frost and Fire

returned with his herd, about twenty horses, running loose, and being driven by his assistant and his dog. In a little while he had picked out seven horses, saddled the three that we should ride first, collected our little amount of luggage and tied it on another horse; and then he chose each horse for its particular rider.

Then, in the saddle, he thought of a possible need upon our part for whips—he already had one, a typical Icelandic whip—one with short stock richly ferruled and with long strap and lash. He went into a store and bought a long rattan reed, cut it into two, and gave each of us a half. My whip did good service for the entire trip, and now, still in my possession, it serves to recall with vividness some of my experiences in that far-away island.

All is ready. The four riderless horses are separated from the rest of the herd, and without bridle run ahead of us, kept in the chosen route by guide and dog. Thus at length, after a sleepless night and a breakfastless morning, we, astride little Icelandic horses turned our backs upon the sea and faced the interior to experience—we knew not what.

CHAPTER VI.

Across the Island

It was at 8:45 o'clock that the signal of readiness was given. With a little help our guide, Mr. Pall Jansson, of San Lanesi Farm, Blonduos, succeeded in getting the four horses that for the time being were to be without rider, but which later were to serve their turn as burden-bearers, separated from the rest of the herd, and started on the path leading to the south. In this first work, and all through the trip, his dog was an important member of our party.

The Icelandic dog is the farmer's best friend, almost having human sagacity. It is of medium size, with a heavy coat of clean hair, and gentle, pleading brown eyes. He seems instinctively to know his master's will, and thus is of incalculable service to him in caring for his sheep, herding his cattle, and driving his horses. On this trip our dog never for a moment lost his alertness. He kept the path or way cleared of all stray animals by racing ahead and chasing them to the right or left over rugged hummocks or rocky wastes for a quarter of a mile or more, and then he would come back immediately to help our guide in caring for the horses that were running loose before us.

Mr. Walley and I are both in high spirits, and we feel a sense of pride in our cavalcade, composed of seven horses, a dog, a guide, and ourselves. Though our guide could not talk with us except by signs, we felt that we would find each other companionable. But in very few places could we ride side by side, and a good part of the time we were so far separated from each other that conversation, except at very infrequent intervals, was scarcely possible. Mr. Walley left it to me to get desired information from, and to give additional direction to our guide, at times no great pleasure to me, accommodating, courteous, and anxious as he was at all times.

And so we started, with barking of dog, and shouting of guide and temporary assistants. When we reached the elevation above the fjord shore a curlew, with a joyful cry, welcomed us. Its song consisted of a *"kirriwirriwirri"* trill, a series of distinct notes, rather shrill in quality, and varying in pitch. The curlew is a bird, or fowl, considerably larger than a dove, and has a long neck, and a long hooked bill.

The curlew that gave us greeting on this morning would sit on a rock or hummock until we would come near to it, or if at times it happened to be a few yards from our path it would wait until we had passed, and then it would rise on wing and swoop down near us and on to another hummock or rock fifty or seventy-five yards ahead, giving that chattering *"kirriwirriwirri"* song of greeting. At first it seemed half musical, and it was interesting to watch the dog at times turn from the horses to give chase to the curlew. Later in the day the song seemed like mockery, and the fact that the dog could not catch the bird was exasperating to us. Not only this day, but almost throughout the entire trip there was at least one curlew at a time following. I do not know, but perhaps in their bird councils it has been planned that each one must do duty over one's own section, or *beat,* and thus see to it that the overland tourist of Iceland shall never get lonely!

The way is only a path, but for the first ten

The Land of Frost and Fire

miles or so of the trip there is a rather excellent roadbed for carriages; but there are as yet no carriages in northern Iceland, save two or three to do a little service in the immediate environs of a coast town or two. So, when noting the telephone poles in the far interior, the furniture of the homes, the lumber used in the houses, and knowing that all this was brought from the coast towns by these little horses, I feel much interested in them. They carry their master on their back where other horses could scarcely go; they carry his produce to the coast and bring back from the sea his provisions and other supplies; and they give their master his last ride when incased in his rude coffin, he lies across the back of one of his horses, supported by a man on either side—a ride out amid the sighs and tears of his loved ones; a ride to the quiet, windowless palace of those who come not back again.

One of the first sights of interest on the trip were the fishers at Salmon River. Here were a number of salmon just pulled from the stream that were at least two feet long. We met one of the happy fishermen on his horse with the fruits of his labor across his shoulder. He seemed proud that we should want his picture, not knowing that it was the fish, and not he, that especially appealed to us.

A menace to all tourists in Iceland are its unbridged streams. These are numerous, usually swift-flowing, and, being glacier-fed, are subject to sudden rise on a bright, sun-shiny day. In many places quicksands are to be found in the river-courses; so it is strongly urged that no one unacquainted with the country undertake a trip through it without a competent guide. On this day we forded six rivers, in three of which I got my feet wet, and in one of which my horse stumbled on the rocky bottom and came near precipitating me headlong into the stream. As it was, I simply measured the water while still astride my horse and while he was with difficulty recovering himself. My clothes were wet and my shoes were filled with water. I did not mind it much in the middle of the day, but when the chill of that evening fell there came with it a numbness and coldness and cramps that resulted in extreme discomfort and misery.

In one place we rode for a mile or two through a region of lava and black sand-heaps where

The Land of Frost and Fire

evidently at one time was an active volcano. Lakes, mountains, brown, bleak, and far-stretching moorlands, and marshes in turn, or simultaneously, gave variety to the landscape.

At intervals of every two or three hours, on reaching a grassy spot, a halt would be called, that our horses might "pick" for a few minutes; and this picking was all the food that the animals got while on the trip. I understand that they feed no grain on this island. I know that they raise none. On dismounting, the reins were thrown down over and in front of the horses' heads, and they had been trained to consider themselves hitched when the reins were hanging thus. There is very little opportunity to hitch a horse in Iceland. Seldom are trees found, and there are no fences except the sod walls about the cluster of buildings at each farm. So the people resort to other ways of hitching. If a horse is inclined to wander away when left alone, one way of hitching him is to place him alongside of another horse, but facing the opposite direction; then they are hitched to the crupper of each other's saddle. Thus hitched, it is almost impossible to have a runaway, for neither one can

The Land of Frost and Fire

run while the other has to go backward. At night they tie the two front feet of a horse tight together, if they want to find him quickly in the morning. And such treatment does not seem to interfere in the least with the serviceableness of the horse. He is ready next day for fifty or seventy miles of travel, and thus for several days in succession.

We passed a number of sod houses and a few sod villages, but did not stop. We had no lunch, therefore did not need to take time to eat. Without sleep the night before and with no food for the day, the ride grew in bitter experience as the day advanced, so that when the thirteen and a-half hours had ended I could say, without need of any qualification, that it was an *awful ride*.

Not a bush or a tree did we see, and no songbird was anywhere to cheer us. But flowers were everywhere, even in the clefts of rocks, and in many places there was a rank growth of grass. In only a few places did we see snow on our first day, and what we saw was high up in depressions on some of the mountain ranges. Pestiferous flies swarmed about us at times with an affectionate clinging that was irritating in the extreme.

The Land of Frost and Fire

About the middle of the afternoon our guide noticed that two of the horses had lost shoes, so he called a halt at a sod house, and, securing aid, proceeded to place shoes where needed. (A guide must always carry horseshoes with him).

While he was thus engaged, my friend and I tried to get off our horses—a difficult thing to do without falling. Then, stumbling to a couple of hummocks, we sat down and held a council of misery. Said I: "Mr Walley, twice in my life I have been very foolish; but I want you to record a resolution that I now make: If ever I get to the end of this trip there will be no long horseback ride again for me!" And then he made confession. Said he: "In England I often ride for an hour or two, and enjoy it; but this, *ah, this ride!* I am on the verge of tears! I fear a nervous prostration!" Then he told me that he had not been on horseback since he had had a surgical operation performed in which a bone had been removed from his knee. And then I feared for him—and also for myself. We are now only midway in the first day, and four more days like unto it are to follow, if we survive!

The Land of Frost and Fire

We had lost no time in our riding. Our guide was in a hurry, but fast riding was a punishment to us. I *couldn't* keep up with him, and Mr. Walley just *wouldn't* make his horse go, but followed "afar off," satisfied simply to keep in sight of us.

But we must not linger in description of the last few hours of this day; the very thought is painful to me. Suffice it to say that at 10:15 p. m. I saw our guide, far ahead of us, stop, turn about, and ride slowly back to meet me. He tried to tell me that we must hurry forward to ferry the head of a fjord in order to find lodging for the night. We were then at the sod wall of a farmhouse. When Mr. Walley came up, we together decided that we would go no farther, if only these people would take us in. By signs and leadings I made known our decision to our guide. He at first shook his head, but finally led us to the front of the sod house, above the door of which, on a wooden lintel, was the word "Thorstadur"—it was the name of the farm. And there we stood face to face with a woman of about fifty years and an attractive girl of about twenty years, both straight and

Steaming Hot Springs   Guide and Dog   Partially Dried Up Lake

dignified in bearing and wearing *hufas*. They listened to our plea. We were led through a passageway between walls of sod about five feet high, on which hung saddles and bridles. Soon we reached a passage crossing this one at right angles. To turn to the left would probably be to enter the kitchen; to go straight forward we would find the living-room and "bad-stofa," or bedroom, combined. We turn to the right, pass a little sod-walled room, and then enter the special guest-chamber that the exterior of the house would never suggest as present here.

This room had a wooden floor, curtains at the windows, pictures on the walls, chairs, narrow bed, center-table and books and was quite cozy, indeed. The ladies retired from the room and the guide went to hobble his horses for the night. Left alone, I began to remove shoes and socks, that I might change to drier footwear. When midway in making the change the young lady came in, without knocking, to set the table for supper! It was an embarrassing moment for me, but she was too modest even to note the cause of my embarrassment. I hid my feet as best I could under my chair during this visit of hers, and

The Land of Frost and Fire

when next she came in I was ready to give her my shoes and socks to take to the fire that I knew was somewhere about the place, to be dried. They were returned to me next morning in good condition.

Formerly in Iceland guests and family occupied the same sleeping apartment, and I understand that in many parts of the island the same practice is necessitated even today. But at no place where we stopped did we find such conditions obtaining. And for this I was thankful.

The table this evening, or night, was set with clean linen, cutlery, and dishes, and, to our surprise, the food was plentiful in quantity and variety, and was quite palatable. It consisted of white and black bread, fresh eggs, milk, bologna, sardines, fresh salmon, dried mutton, butter, cheese, sweet cakes, and coffee—a most delicious and satisfying meal after our long, almost unbroken fast of about thirty hours. We ate by the light of the afterglow at about eleven o'clock, no other light being necessary.

My friend had insisted on carrying his cap in his pocket all day instead of wearing it, and the sun and wind had so tanned his face that his

The Land of Frost and Fire

complexion now was quite ruddy, and the skin had begun to scale off and his lips were cracked and bleeding. We were too wearied to want to talk, so sat dozing while our beds were being supplied with pure, fresh linen.

When all was ready, Mr. Walley came shambling to where I sat, and, placing his arm about my shoulder, said in tremulous tones (as though he felt that he might not have opportunity to say it in the morning, and I, too, half feared he would not), "I hope you will forgive me for getting you into this dreadful experience." I assured him it was all right and that the worst was over, notwithstanding we had yet four days to be in the saddle. But I nevertheless had some misgivings about it. Then he went to his little room, and soon in our narrow beds we gave ourselves over to "tired nature's sweet restorer," and forgot the woes of the day in dreams of fairer climes.

CHAPTER VII.

Second Day in the Interior

AFTER a most refreshing sleep, I am recalled to consciousness by the gentle opening of my door and the beautiful young lady, with *hufa* on her head and bearing a tray with steaming coffee, two kinds of cake, and bread, came softly to my bedside, and, drawing up a chair, placed the tray on it, and then retired without further attempt at speech than a simple morning greeting. I thought it was my breakfast that she had brought, and ate and drank heartily. It seemed nice to be waited on thus.

Then, rising and preparing for a continuation of our trip, I found Mr. Walley apparently ready also, but shuddering at the thought of a possible repetition of the experience of yesterday. But imagine our surprise when the young woman of the home began to set the table for our breakfast; and a meal as sumptuous as the one on the evening before was soon before us. The only trouble was, we had eaten and drunk too

The Land of Frost and Fire

freely of the first serving—like the man who ate his fill of soup, not knowing anything else was to follow, and when he saw one delicious course follow another, but of which he could not eat, sat ashamed, chafed and angry at his evident loss. The lodging and two meals cost us three kroner (about eighty-five cents) apiece.

Twice in my story I have referred to women wearing *hufas*. It is well that I now explain. All Icelandic women from about twelve years old and upward wear on their heads a little circle of knit material, black and about five inches in diameter. In the center of this circle, and a continuation of the knit work, is an extended portion like the finger of a glove, but about six inches long; to the end of the extension is fastened a silk tassel, a foot in length. At the union of the tassel with the knit-work there is always a ferrule of silver or gold, sometimes highly ornamented and costly; the ferrule is usually about two inches in length. The effect when upon the head of the wearer is quite pleasing, suggesting modesty and a semi-scholastic appearance. On festal occasions the women wear a high, white ornamental head-garment instead of the *hufa*.

Though very sore, I am ready at 9:45 a.m., and our second day's ride begins. When we had proceeded about a mile, Mr. Walley discovered that he had lost an important piece of his camera. We sent our guide back to find it, while we tried to hold our herd together. After waiting some time, I turned the herd over to my friend and rode back to assist in the search. Soon I found the missing part, and then we were ready to move on. But we had tried to tell our guide not to move so rapidly as on the day before.

When we started, and until noon, the air was warm and sultry, and at times a light rain fell. The day was cloudy throughout, and from noon on we faced a cold wind. We crossed streams at least fifteen times, but, having learned from yesterday's experience, I kept my feet dry by drawing them up to the back of my horse. We passed a number of good farms, each with its cluster of sod houses, the first of importance being Stadur, where there is a telephone station and a church.

About noon we began climbing steadily into

The Land of Frost and Fire

the interior. Our path was rugged, and at times we descended into river-courses by steep and slippery banks where safety suggested that we dismount.

Throughout the afternoon the snow-covered mountain, Banda, looms majestic to the right of us. The numerous streams at times present beautiful cascades and falls. Now we find ice and snowdrifts that have not yet yielded to the summer warmth. Occasionally we follow river-courses where the canyons are deep and induce a strange thrill because of our nearness to the rim. There were not so many curlews to-day. I saw three eider-ducks. In one of the streams I saw a primitive water-wheel which was turned by the water's passing at its side, and the upright post to which the wheel was fastened led up to a small hopper where whatever was to be ground was fed to the crushing-stones.

At three o'clock I saw the first bushes yet seen on the trip, and here I heard for the first time in Iceland a song-bird. A little later we rode across a small glacier, and soon were in front of a refuge-house. In many places along the way to-day we found high heaps of stones to mark the way for travelers in winter-time when the snow is very deep. Nobody has permanent residence in the refuge-houses; they are simply shelter from the storm for man and beast until they dare venture out again.

From one of the high ridges that we crossed we saw a beautiful panorama of hill, mountain, barren plain, rocky ravine, and dashing river. The largest river that we crossed to-day is the Nord. At the last river that we crossed, my friend, weary and taking his time, had dropped so far behind as not to see where we had crossed. Attempting to cross where he thought it best, his horse mired to the depth of half his body, and only with difficulty could he be extricated. We learned of this only on waiting for him and noting his dripping horse and garments.

About ten o'clock in the evening we entered what the natives called the "forest". It is of dwarf birch and covers several square miles of a wide-stretching river bottom; in it there is scarcely a tree over three inches in diameter or ten feet high. And here again I hear song-birds. How much a bird seems to need a tree or bush! There is no certain path through the "forest," and our

A Fair Virginian in Ordinary Icelandic Dress

Icelandic Maiden in Festive Attire

The Land of Frost and Fire

way is found with some difficulty. A half mile beyond is Norstunga, our destination for the night. At this place is a frame house, a small church, and a bridge, the materials for all having been brought from the coast on the backs of the little horses, or were in part dragged by them. It is 10:45 p.m.

We found everybody in bed except one man down at the river, waist deep in the water, fishing. Our approach in the weird half-light and quiet of that night reminded me of the approach of "night riders" to the home of unsuspecting victims. Two beautiful girls in nightdress and slippers came out in response to the repeated knocking of our guide. Then the man of the house and one who was evidently his wife, a queenly woman in appearance and bearing, appeared. We were ushered into a comfortable and well-furnished room, and immediately they began preparations for our supper.

And while we waited, three other men arrived, two of whom had been with us on the boat. These two had undertaken to make the trip across the island by sharing a bicycle between them. They started on their trip at Bordeyri,

The Land of Frost and Fire

in opposition to the wishes and counsel of all on board who knew Iceland. All had said, "You can't go across Iceland on a bycicle." But the Scotchman, who owned the wheel, persisted in the thought that he could do it and in the determination that he would do it, and his English companion championed the enterprise. But tonight they came in without the wheel; they had three ponies and a guide instead. Upon our asking about the wheel, the owner said, "Aye, such roads! such rivers! I got tired carrying my wheel and shoes above my head as I crossed the streams. And then the fording was so rough that my feet are so bruised that I can hardly walk! I left my wheel back yonder at a farm-house with word to send it back to Scotland at the first opportunity. Aye, we find the ponies surer." (After reaching my home a few months later, I received a letter from this gentleman, stating that his wheel had come to him all right.)

At twelve o'clock midnight we were seated at an excellent meal, and we ate again by the simple light of the after-glow, and then immediately sought the rest we so much needed after the stress of thirteen hours in the saddle.

CHAPTER VIII.

The Third and the Fourth Day in the Interior.

Last night I again had a clean bed to myself and slept *on* feathers and *under* feathers. I rose early to write the story of yesterday. On making an inventory of my aches and pains I am emphatic that to-day the rate of speed will be at the minimum.

We were late starting this morning, it being 10:20 o'clock when we mounted our horses. Then we separated company from the late-comers of last night and began our weary way.

To-day we crossed immediately a bridge, one of two that will accommodate us on this stage of our trip, and one of three or four on the whole overland trip. In a little while we sighted a number of steaming hot springs, a novelty to my companion, but not to one who had previously seen the Yellowstone Park of my own country. Nevertheless, the sight was beautiful and interesting. The largest river to-day was the seething

The Land of Frost and Fire

glacier-colored Hvita. Surely, had there been no bridge here we had not been able to cross it.

In the course of to-day we passed near Starholt, where there is a church. We later passed immediately in front of Lunder, where there is a church and a few graves—the first grave I had seen since leaving the coast. The way was rough throughout the day; the weather was not so cold as yesterday, but we had some drizzling mist-like rain, and later, bright sunshine. Sometimes we followed an indistinct path over rocky ridges, and then we would be picking our way through miry sulphur marshes, or following no path at all. Occasionally we would pass where the path had been worn about two feet deep and barely wide enough for the feet of our horses to pass each other in it. To escape injury I had to throw my feet over my horse's back. But even with all my care, on rounding a rocky ledge the path was so narrow that my knee was crushed against the rock wall with such violence as to cause an involuntary cry of pain to escape me.

Toward evening when we began to ascend a river-course between mountain ranges I felt sure that our guide was in error, and, experiment-

The Land of Frost and Fire

ing with my compass, I felt additional certainty in the matter, and tried to tell him that he was wrong; but either he did not understand me, or did not care to understand. He simply said, "*Yau,*" (which means "yes"), and rode on. To add to my annoyance, my English friend just would not whip his horse to keep up with me. So the guide indicated for me to get behind and switch-up his horse for him. I have much of this to do, and it wearies me nearly as much as my riding. But we have planned an easy day and shall reach our destination early. So in the late afternoon we permit our horses to pick their way as best they can over hummocks and rocks while we note the beautiful river-courses in the black lava-rock mountains, with here and there a waterfall of no mean significance, until 5:45 p.m. Holt is reached; here two hours later we retire that we may get the rest necessary to endure the to-morrow's trip of anticipated hardships.

In the light night I awoke to hear voices in undertone just beneath my window; then there was quiet, stealthy moving about; but several times they came back and low conversations were heard at my window. Had I not been in Iceland, I'd have suspected intentional mischief; as it was, it simply created an air of mystery that I was not able to understand, even next morning.

We wanted an early start this time. The hostess served a delicious breakfast in which I ate the sweetest and most palatable fish that I had ever tasted. I do not know the Icelandic name for the fish, but I think the English name is "char." It is a species of salmon, but much better than even fresh salmon, to my taste.

Before starting, at 8:15 a.m., the lady of the home explained in signs and Icelandic names a map of her country that was on the wall of the room in which we ate; and then she took us out and pointed out by name some of the jokulls that were seen towering near or far.

I felt somewhat anxious to get onto my horse this morning. Our way led over a high and rocky mountain. But almost everywhere were flowers—silver-leaved lady's mantle, lady's bedstraw, grass of Parnassus, sea-pink, saxiphrage, buttercup, wild thyme, spotted orchis, and other varieties that I cannot name. For about an

The Land of Frost and Fire

hour to-day we had to have a local guide, as there was no path to follow. On a high ridge near us and silhouetted against the sky a few ravens sat and watched us, it seemed with hungry interest. Until noon Ok jokull was in plain view to our left; also the Skjaldsbreid jokull, near which we rode while keeping Sula mountain on our right. After crossing several small steaming sulphur streams, and climbing wearily the rocky slope we reached at noon the highest point attained on our trip. Here the heavy branching moss was about a foot deep and strong enough to support the weight of a man— it seemed like walking over a heavy brussels carpet.

Leaning against a great rock and studying the snow-capped mountains and upper ice-fields extending for miles backward and skyward, the traveler is apt to be reminded of Switzerland, save that here shrubbery and tree-growth are lacking. The air is pure and bracing, bringing a message of health from the heights, and slightly scented with the flowers that in the short summer seem doing double duty swinging their censers to perfume the breezes for the poor natives of this land of the long winter night.

Just ahead of us is a great depression now filled with water, forming what would be a beautiful lake were it fringed with grasses and ferns. One time it was the crater of a vast and terrible volcano. Riding around this we spent half the afternoon in winding and zigzagging down the farther slope, sometimes over dangerously steep and rough places, over great stretches of volcanic sand and by scroll-like lava beds, rent in great crevices, or fissures, and everywhere showing forth the story of awful fire-struggle in ages past, and with here and there steam-jets pregnant with sulphur even to-day.

About the middle of the afternoon we reach a great depressed area in the farther end of which there is yet a lake of considerable size. At some seasons the water covers many times the area it occupies at present. We ride for an hour over soft-yielding, moist sand skirting the water's edge. Then we climb a steep ridge and only a little way ahead we sight "Lady's Seat," somewhere beyond which is the Valley of Thingvellir.

A Common Experience When Travelling in Iceland

On the Logberg
Thingvellir Lake

in which is to be our destination for the night. It is now six o'clock.

"Lady's Seat" is a semi-isolated height running out with a gradual incline upward, from the ridge on which we now are, for a few hundred yards, very narrow at the beginning, but gradually widening as you proceed, and ending suddenly with a precipitous height of several hundred feet above the plain. Dismounting and turning our horses over to the guide, we pick our way out over the deep springy moss to the end of the "seat." What a scene! Grassy meadow just in front with a number of horses "picking" and a number of men and women lounging about. Beyond the meadow is the wide-stretching valley, the historical center of the whole island. On the farther side of the valley is the beautiful island-dotted lake. All around the valley and lake are precipitous cliff-walls from twenty-five feet to several hundred feet in height.

When we came from "Lady's Seat" the guide had already taken the horses down to the meadow; and we were glad, for the way down was very rough—rude steps had been formed of big

The Land of Frost and Fire

boulders. It was difficult to walk down; riding was scarcely possible. I was told that there are only four places where entrance can be made into the valley—one at each of the cardinal points of the compass.

Then we rode for two hours over a desolate lava-bed (only passing a few farms in that time), with great fissures here and there yawning at either side, twenty to fifty feet deep, in the bottoms of some of which I could see water, as my horse trod within a foot or two of the edge. A struggling dwarf birch growth lies twisted over the rocks, scarcely finding enough nourishment to give it strength to raise its head.

After eight o'clock we reached our destination for the night—Thingvellir Hotel; and here we found interested friends to greet us. They had come out to this place after the boat had reached Reykjavik. We were glad to see them, but not proud that they should see us as we found ourselves after our hard four days; for my friend's face was red and blistered, and I felt too weary to hold my head erect. But thus we were compelled to run the gauntlet of their interested scrutiny.

CHAPTER IX.

The Valley of Thingvellir.

The valley into which we have entered is the historic center of the whole island. When the Althing, the government of Iceland, was established in 930 A. D., here was its seat, and here it remained several hundred years. To this valley the people of the whole land were expected to come once every year to tarry for two weeks. In that fortnight controversies were settled, cases were tried, sentences were pronounced, and executions were carried out, relating to the year ending; and new laws and regulations might be made for the year beginning. Any man might come and plead his own case before the Althing.

To the visitor, familiar in part with this history, this valley, bearing evidences on every hand of awful cataclysms and terrors in geologic ages, becomes the arena of struggle between men before the tribunal of justice, where the fires of hate and strife were either quenched, or one or both of the parties executed. What jargon of tongues in this annual gathering—men and women who have fled to this place as to a city of refuge to claim the protection of the council, and pleading with the eloquence of tears and sobs for recognition of their pitiable plight! And men and women, criminal in every intent and act, waiting in dogged and sullen silence the sentence—and also the execution that must surely follow the awful arraignment in court! For, in those days, it is said, before the session of the Althing had ended and the people had dispersed to their homes, the execution of every sentence was carried out in the presence of the people.

Yes, Thingvellir is to Iceland to-day what the Forum is to Rome and the Acropolis to Athens. And when the Icelanders celebrated their thousandth anniversary of history in 1874, it was to Thingvellir that every eye and heart turned as the fitting place for the crowning feature of the event. And though it is fifty kilometers from Reykjavik, and though they had as guest of honor the King of Denmark, their own king, they took him on horseback to the place of their national beginnings.

The Land of Frost and Fire

This valley surrounded by high mountains, an area once lowered suddenly by the hand of the Almighty, and to-day with its deep and fearful chasms, its blasted vegetation, its steaming hot springs, might suggest that it is in awful poise, or suspense, liable again to sink until perhaps buried in the bosom of the earth. What a place was this in which to mete out justice when both the criminal and the judge were in the same valley of decision—and that whole valley itself mysteriously held from sinking into oblivion! Of course, the fact that it has not sunk deeper within the history of man gives unusual boldness to the visitor; but the evidences are on every hand that this that is now called a valley did sink at least seventy-five feet and then stopped,—to sink no farther? Who knows?

Of this valley of erstwhile terrors we shall note a few things of special interest. On the evening of my arrival I walked out a little way from the hotel, but was soon stopped by deep, yawning fissures in the rocky earth; and far down I could hear the gurgling, lapping water like a great fiend reveling in delightful but forbidden gratification of desire. Then looking about me

The Land of Frost and Fire

in the weird light, I concluded to postpone further investigations until the morning.

The following morning found me ready early to begin sight-seeing. I first go to the Logberg, the tribunal rock-island, where the judges of the Althing sat in council—the Areopagus of the Icelanders. There is only one way in which to reach the Logberg. It is an island formed by the separating of one large fissure into two, each of which is nearly as large as the one of which it forms a part. The island formed by these two fissures is probably fifty feet wide at the widest place, and it is probably one hundred yards long (dimensions are given from memory and may vary materially from being accurate). At one end of the island the displacement of a great rock and its lodgment in the fissure forms a natural bridge over which one may walk to the Logberg.

On this island one must walk very carefully, for while on one part of it there is a luxuriant growth of forget-me-nots and other flowers, one must be careful in approaching the sides of the island. Here are the great fissures, ten to fifteen feet wide and forty to fifty feet deep to water, and with a depth of water in some places

The Land of Frost and Fire

of fifty or more feet. Standing on the edge of such a chasm is by no means a pleasure-giving experience to most people, and, because of a prenatal event for my friend, he is quite ill at ease.

Onto a jutting rock in one of the fissures referred to, it is said, criminals, sentenced here to die, were thrown to break their backs; and then their limp bodies would fall to the dark depths where the water with demon-like gurgle would swallow them up and hide them away forever from the sight of those they had wronged. Think of it! Just here where I stand the accusation was brought against him in the Althing—maybe with tears he pleaded for mercy, but he is adjudged guilty; he is sentenced to die. He is now in the hands of the executioner. There is no dangling at the end of a rope for people to see him, and then in the night to dream of the contorted face and writhing body; no bleeding, headless trunk with headsman wiping his gory ax, the lingering, subconscious memory of which to cause children to gasp and cringe in sleep. No! A quick movement on the verge of the abyss—then—*gone forever!*

The Land of Frost and Fire

As has already been said, here, in the year 1000 A. D., by action of the Althing, Christianity was made the religion of the land. And then began its literary age resulting in the best of its *Sagas* and *Eddas*. And here were witnessed deeds of valor and many contests of gory renown.

But to-day, how different! Think not of deeds of blood; look not into the abyss of groans and despair-laden tradition. But rather linger among the flowers so profuse in growth and rich in color; and though growing on soil oft drenched with human blood, let their beauty and fragrance point to the "Rose of Sharon" and the "Lily of the Valley," whose life-teachings were memorialized here nine hundred years ago in government decree; and let that beauty and fragrance tell of a future grand in hope.

A merry party of natives, men and women, gallop along the road leading by the lake. I envy their horsemanship. Later I try to penetrate farther over the moss and straggling low bushes beyond the Logberg, but finding that it requires much care because of the ruggedness of the surface and because of fissures, large and small, I return to look at the church

The Almannagja

Hecla

and parsonage which, either in themselves, or in the buildings that preceded them, bear a close relationship to much of historic interest in the region. The church is quite small, eighteen by twenty-eight feet, and is a frame structure. But notwithstanding its insignificance of size and structure, kings have stood within it. By it are a few graves. The parsonage is not an inviting building, but it is good, for the interior of Iceland. It is a wooden building.

I next visit the Almannagja, or "All-Men's-Rift," a great rift, or chasm, at one edge of the sunken valley, and near the Logberg. When the valley sank, the river Oxara, that formerly flowed into and through this region, then necessarily flowed into the rift, or chasm. Though the rim of the chasm on the valley side was lowered seventy-five, or more, feet below the outer rim (that did not sink), the chasm itself was still much deeper. Through this chasm, after the plunge resulting in beautiful falls of possibly one hundred feet, the river flows for about a quarter of a mile and then makes a sudden turn through the inner rim and out into the valley, and a

The Land of Frost and Fire

little later flows into the beautiful island-dotted lake of Thingvellir.

Just where the river turns through the inner rim, there is a sort of whirlpool, which, through the centuries, has been known as the "drowning-pool." Tradition says that in this pool women who were adjudged unfaithful to their husbands were sentenced to be drowned. And then these heights were covered with people to witness the executions, hence the name, "All-Men's-Rift," or "Almannagja."

Seated on this rift, where to-day wild thyme and other flowers grow in rich profusion, but from which place, if the traditions be true, one could plainly have witnessed the executions in the "drowning-pool," or at the "blood-stone" on the Logberg, I dwell for a time in that dreamy, dreadful past—and then urge myself out of the reverie to look at the present scene. In front of me is the Almannagja, with the rushing Oxara and the frowning west wall; to the north are desolate, somber-hued mountains; to the east is the valley, and hazy heights are in the distance; to the south—ah, here is beauty! The historic places already referred to are in the foreground,

The Land of Frost and Fire

beyond is the glassy lake mirroring in strong shadow the islands that rise from its bosom, and at the farther side the mind sees the river Sog spring lightly from the pent-up valley and carry the crystal treasures of its mother-lake to hide them forever in intermingling with the vast and open sea.

CHAPTER X.

Last Day On Horseback.

When we thought we were ready to leave the hotel at Thingvellir, and were on our horses, it was discovered that our dog had not been fed. And of such value had he proven himself that to look into his pleading, almost human eyes and know that he was hungry at the beginning of a six or eight hours' trip in which he was to serve us well, was sufficient to make us willing to tarry an hour, if need be, to secure him food, even though it should make us late in reaching Reykjavik, our destination for that night.

Slightly past noon we started; and soon we crossed the bridge over the Oxara, just below the "drowning-pool." Here we met a train of horses bearing lumber into the interior. Each horse carried two bundles, one on either side; and these two bundles were tied together and the uniting cord or chain was thrown across the saddle, or pannier. The front ends of the bundles were elevated above the horse's head while

The Land of Frost and Fire

the rear ends dragged upon the ground. Sometimes a very heavy stick of timber is carried between two horses.

Almost immediately after crossing the stream we began a remarkable ascent. Up through the high rock-wall left exposed when the valley sank there is a deep narrow cleft, in places barely wide enough for vehicles to pass through. While the ascent is rather steep, it is gradual. When the road from the capital was pushed through to this valley, here was the only place that it was possible to enter. Nature opened the passage, and then man graded it and put up protecting walls and pillars. It is indeed a romantic and exceedingly interesting gateway to Thingvellir through which we are now passing outward. On either side high, dark walls of rock, heavy shadows on the path, pretty flowers in nooks and on narrow ledges—all so impressive. And when we reached the western summit and turned to look down that great crack in the wall through which we had just ridden, we were grateful that the fissure had made it possible for us to get out of the valley, and that it did not close its terrible jaws while we were passing through it. We entered

The Land of Frost and Fire

Thingvellir by walking down a very rocky cleft, or ravine, and left it as just described.

After a lingering view of the valley from this most excellent viewpoint, we move forward on this last stage of our horseback riding. If all goes well, we shall reach our destination by early twilight. The distance is scarcely more than thirty-five miles and the road is excellent—a splendid carriage-road of recent construction, about the only one that I saw in Iceland.

We thought that by walking our horses the greater part of the way we would still have plenty of time for our trip; but later we found it would require the usual rapid movement if we would reach Reykjavik at the designated hour.

Though the road is good, it proves to be a monotonous and very wearying ride. Then the flies, or gnats, are so very annoying—getting into our nostrils, mouths, ears, and eyes—and very tenacious in their devotion to us. There are few grassy plots, but flowers apparently everywhere—even on what seemed endless waste lands.

For about one-third of the distance between Thingvellir and Reykjavik there stretches out in

The Land of Frost and Fire

bigness and loneliness of desolation the "Mossfell Moor." In the glare of the afternoon, notwithstanding the little flowers and the occasional trill of the curlew, the spirits are depressed. It seems as though nature would say to all, "Enter not here," were this highway not already established. And along this road are mute evidences of the awful winters that reign here supreme. At intervals of every few rods are rock-built pillars or pyramids eight or ten feet high, to mark the road when deep snows lie on the moor; and that there may be no doubt as to the side on which the road lies, there is a rock at the top of each pillar that is made to project toward the road. And two or three refuge-houses are along the way—uninviting in appearance, but a haven of hope to one caught here in a merciless winter storm.

As we rode over this bleak stretch of melancholy-inducing waste and thought of the gathering winter tempest, when even the rocks would seem to ring in challenge to the smiting blast, and when the storm-king would shout his commands from Hengill Mountain, and the air would be filled with blinding powder of snow—ah, what then could a poor stray wayfarer do on **Moss-fell Moor**! Many lives are said to have been lost where we now ride. Said Mr. Walley, "I can't help thinking of a phrase of Cardinal Newman's hymn, 'Lead, Kindly Light'; it is this: 'O'er moor and fen.'" And then we repeated the last stanza of that sweet hymn:

"So long thy power hath kept me,
 Sure it still will lead me on
O'er moor and fen, o'er crag and torrent,
 Till the night is gone;
And blest with the morn those angel faces smile,
 Which I have loved long since, and lost awhile."

At one point on our way we caught sight of Hecla, that king of volcanoes in Iceland, but to-day wearing a cloak and cap of snow. It is not far from the southern coast, and is about centrally located in the longitude of the island.

When about half of our distance was covered we reached the summit of a rise in the road and far to the west I saw the great shining ocean. Almost involuntarily my cap was removed from my head, and I said in joyous exclamation, "Yonder is the sea; and beyond is home!" And then

A Scene in Reykjavik

West-mann Islands

The Land of Frost and Fire

I felt a strange tugging at the tense strings of an emotion that must exist somewhere in the heart of every man. And the people of this land claim to have found that home for me!

At the same time far to the northwest is seen Snaefell's jokull—eighty miles away, yet not looking more than twenty. (Distance is very deceptive in these northern latitudes.) New vigor seemed induced by the sight of the sea and the thought of home. So for the rest of the way we rode more rapidly. The heaviest rainfall of our trip was encountered near its close, but it did not delay us. We were considered very fortunate in escaping so well.

Just a little before reaching the capital city we crossed another bridge, and in an hour or less time, at 8:30 p.m. we were riding through the streets of Reykjavik to a resting-place in the splendid hotel bearing the same name as the city itself. Here we parted temporarily from our guide who had to take his horses outside the city limits that he might find grass for them in the night. But we strongly urged him to return to take supper with us, as a kind of joyous recognition of his services rendered us. We waited for him;

but he did not come. We shall know why in the morning.

After supper, the *Botnia* not being in the harbor, I went to the Hotel Iceland for the night. It was an evening of repose, and a night of satisfying, refreshing sleep.

CHAPTER XI.

REYKJAVIK.

It was late (ten o'clock) when I arose the next morning, and, feeling somewhat the effects of my five days on horseback, I determined to devote myself leisurely to seeing the sights of the city. I first went to find my English friend. Our guide soon appeared to receive his pay and to say good-by. He was visibly perturbed. An interpreter said that he had lost his dog. In the city the dog had strayed or had been enticed away from him. How would the man be able to take all his horses back over the almost trackless waste without his dog? He missed him in the early evening and had hunted for him until nearly midnight, this being the reason our guide could not come to our supper. He had renewed and continued the search in the early morning hours. It was hard on our guide to lose his dog, and even we felt that we had lost a friend.

It is no light thing to say good-by to a guide that has served you well; who has led you to sights that please and scenes that awe; who has picked out a path to safety for you where you know there are dangers of quicksand and flood. But we have said it to Pall Jansson, and have watched his retreating figure as he passed into the street and out to his horses and on to his dwelling-place on the northern shore of his bleak island home. He is gone, but he is not, nor shall he ever be, forgotten.

Reykjavik is a town of about twelve thousand people, and in some of its aspects is quite modern. It has some fine streets, pretty homes, good stores, two banks, telephone and telegraph, fairly good sewerage, and gas lighting. Its chief industries are fishing and commerce. Great sheds are filled with fish packed for the markets. In other parts of the city are stone-paved areas on which fish are being dried.

But to-day, after writing many letters, I go to the Senate House, a rather imposing structure, to the Cathedral, and to the Museum; but the last-named place was not open at the hour of my visit. Then I walk the streets and enter stores, surprised at the air of progressiveness that prevails. There are three newspapers published

The Land of Frost and Fire

here; one of them is the "Isafold," the paper having the peculiar manner of printing a serial story (as already referred to) that when it is finished the subscriber has the story in book form by simply clipping out and stitching together.

The *Botnia* came into port this evening about seven o'clock and anchored nearly a half mile from the jetty (there is no pier at Reykjavik). I wanted to go to the boat, but I had difficulty in persuading any boatman to take me, for the sea was rough and the waves were high. But by agreeing to pay more than double the usual price, two men undertook to row me to the *Botnia*. They placed me in the stern of the little boat and indicated that I must steer the vessel—a thing that I never before in my life had attempted to do; and to thread our way among other boats and over boisterous waves was more than enough for one so unskilled as I. But after a few semi-serious blunders on my part we arrived safe, and a feeling of restfulness and security came to me as I climbed the side-ladder of the boat I had left a week earlier at Blonduos, on the northern coast of the island. And on board the *Botnia*, in my own berth, I slept in quiet peace that night.

The Land of Frost and Fire

On shore again next morning at eleven o'clock, I first visit the "Laguar," or hot springs, which can be reached in less than an hour's walk from the landing-place. When I reached the springs I saw every evidence that the water was hot, nevertheless, I wanted to verify my opinion by testing it. When I approached the water I saw a boy that seemed only half-witted watching me, and when I thrust my fingers into the water, but drew them out again with such celerity as surprised even myself, and then saw the unfeigned delight of that boy I knew that I was not mistaken in my surmisings as to his sanity!

This place, because there is no expense for fuel, is made the chief washing-place for Reykjavik; and the stream has been made to pass through convenient permanent channels, and buildings have been erected to serve the people well. When I visited the place there were possibly a dozen women and several men engaged at work washing. Clothes were spread out over large areas or were hanging on lines to dry: A woman once fell into the stream and was scalded to death; and so they had to place curved iron bars over the channels in such positions and arrange-

The Land of Frost and Fire

ment as would permit washing and at the same time protect the persons from falling in.

Near this place is the Leper Hospital. At one time there were many lepers in Iceland; but in recent years there was established this hospital, a large imposing building on the shore of the harbor. So carefully and scientifically have they treated the cases, and dealt with the dread peril, that it is said there are only about fifty inmates now in the institution. And this number, I think, represents the number of lepers on the entire island.

On returning to the city I went to the museum, which in the main is surprisingly good for the far North, and which in its exhibits of ancient native-work in wood and stone and bone are exceptionally fine.

Leaving the museum, I study the architecture of the buildings, which is, ordinarily, severely plain, but in many instances it bears marks of the distinctively artistic. And the people interest me. I see girls and women in their homes, in the stores, or on the streets wearing *hufas* and lamb-skin slippers, and some wearing the beautiful ermine-trimmed eiderdown cloaks. And some of the girls are unmistakably attractive. The men

The Land of Frost and Fire

as a rule wear no distinctive national garment. My experience leads me to say, with no uncertainty in the statement, that I found the Icelander almost universally courteous.

Then I walk to the farther limit of the city studying the view of the bay and of far-off, yet apparently near, Snaefell's jokull, from every vantage viewpoint. Then I return by way of the cemetery to look at the lake and the governor's mansion, and to tarry awhile in the park, or central square, about which the chief public buildings of the city are located. In the center of the park is a statute of Thorwaldson, known as the great Danish sculptor, but who was born of Icelandic parents, at sea. Thorwaldson carved the "Lion of Lucerne" in Switzerland; and his "Twelve Apostles," to be seen in a church in Copenhagen, is one of the world's master-productions. And his great hall of statuary in the same city, containing none but the works of his own hands, is a marvel to any beholder. In an open central court in this Copenhagen hall of statuary, under a bed of ivy, with no marble or bronze above him, sleeps the great sculptor whose statute we have just seen in the park at Reykjavik. The Icelanders do well to claim him, and thus to honor him.

CHAPTER XII.

"Good-by."

At four o'clock in the evening I went again to the boat, and my tour in Iceland was ended. But still I studied the city from the boat. Just a little way from where we lie at anchor are the two small islands, Vithey and Engey. The latter of these two is distinctively the home of the eider-duck, and is said to be a place of unique and unusual interest when the young are hatching and the owners of the island are gathering the down which we value so highly.

Having visited the land, and having associated with and studied the people, I must modify my former conceptions of both very materially. But the same is true of all places, persons, and things— the more we know about them the more must our original thought concerning them be changed. With respect to Iceland my change of thought is all favorable to the land and her people. I am glad for this trip.

At 7:30 p.m., on that evening, July 21, we

The Land of Frost and Fire

weighed anchor to begin our return to Scotland. The twilight was filled with haze, and in the weird after hours the city and the land, receding, seemed swallowed up in a sort of lead-colored mist—the land to be seen once more on the morrow.

The sea was rough and the boat rocked and pitched considerably in the night. And since we had on board about three hundred horses (over a hundred more had been taken on at Reykjavik), I feared for them.

At 6:30 o'clock the next morning we made our last stop before reaching Leith, our starting-point for the trip. It was at the Westmann Islands, lying only a little to the south of the coast of Iceland. Here the sea was too rough for us to get to the town, so we anchored somewhat to the leeward of the great cliffs. These islands are noted for the multitudes of their birds, or sea-fowls, which the natives catch by daring feats, and, it is said, then use the dried oily bodies as fuel in the winter time. The natives also draw up their sheep by means of ropes to the grassy spots on the upper heights for them there to feed.

The Land of Frost and Fire

The quiet of the morning is like a Sunday, and the waves playing against the cliffs make a solemn music, which I think must be continuous here. But we stopped for only an hour and then weighed anchor for our final run to Scotland.

The morning was bright and sunny, and a very fine view of southern Iceland was ours all through that forenoon. I had excellent views of headlands, barren wastes, mountains, and snow-fields extending far inland. I could plainly see Hecla (over 5,000 feet high), Eyjafjalla jokull, and Myrdals jokull. The scene will not be forgotten.

And then came the heavy sea! For nearly two whole days the waves were very boisterous and seemed continually to want to wash the deck of our vessel—and our boat rolled and pitched like a plaything among them. In the hours of the tempest one night a child was born to one of the passengers. A purse of ninety-nine and three-fourths kroner was made up and given to the proud parents; and they named the child "Botnia," in honor of the boat and in recognition of the kindness shown them on it.

This return voyage ranks first for miserable

experiences in all of my seafaring. I was undeniably sea-sick! For thirty-six hours I tasted not a mouthful of food. Sometimes it was with difficulty that I could maintain my place in my berth, because of the rocking and pitching of the boat. In the midst of my distress I sent for my friend of the overland route; and when he had reached my cabin I said, "Mr. Walley, I want you to record another resolution—'When I get home, if that boon be granted me, there will be no more long sea voyaging for me!"

But I love the sea, and even now I have forgotten the serious nature of that vow, and should fortune smile and beckon me, there would be a responsive thrill in answer to the call.

But the memory of those awful days! In thought of them the following not very classic lines (slightly modified) by Joseph Bert Smiley, very aptly express my feelings and pleas:

"*Briny Ocean, ere we part,*
  Give, oh, give me back my heart,
Give me back my walking-gear,
  Give me back my breakfast dear,
Or since that's a vain request,
  Keep it now, and take the rest.

The Land of Frost and Fire

"Briny Ocean, heaving high,
  Kiss me once and let me die,
I've an awful goneness now—
  Cold drops plenty on my brow.
Angry Ocean, rolling by,
  Wash me in, and let me die.

"Briny Ocean, still thy tide.
  As thou rock'st from side to side,
How I wish that I were dead!
  Then thou stand'st me on my head!
Ocean, rock me safe to sleep
  In thy cradle of the deep!"

www.ingramcontent.com/pod-product-compliance
Lightning Source LLC
Chambersburg PA
CBHW021938160426
43195CB00011B/1136